Historic England

Manchester

Jean & John Bradburn

AMBERLEY

About the Author

Jean is a proud Mancunian. She worked in Manchester's Central Library for many years. Recently retired, she is an adult tutor, offering courses in family history. John has numerous production credits in theatre, TV and film. A former BBC and Granada employee, he has worked mainly for the last decade in portrait, film and artscape photography.

Previous publications: *The Bridgewater Canal Through Time*; *Central Manchester Through Time*; *Widnes Through Time*; *Cheetham Hill, Crumpsall, Blackley and Moston Through Time*; and *Runcorn Through the Ages*.

First published 2017

Amberley Publishing
The Hill, Stroud, Gloucestershire, GL5 4EP
www.amberley-books.com

The images on the follwoing pages are from the author's own collection: 3, 14 (lower), 15 (lower), 16, 18 (top), 20 (lower), 29, 32 (lower), 45 (lower), 49, 52 (lower), 53 (lower), 54 (lower), 58 (lower), 73, 81 (lower), 93 (top).

The images on the following pages are © Crown Copyright. Historic England Archive: 12 (upper), 18 (lower), 22 (lower), 57 (upper), 62 (upper) 68, 69, 75,90, 91.

The images on the following pages are © Historic England Archive: 21, 31, 32 (upper), 33, 36, 37, 38, 39, 51 56 (upper), 70, 71, 72 (upper), 74, 76, 77, 80, 81 (upper), 82, 83, 84, 86, 88 (lower), 89, 92, 93 (upper), 94, 95.

All other images , unless indicated otherwise, have been reproduced by permission of the Historic England Archive.

ISBN 978 1 4456 7536 7 (print)
ISBN 978 1 4456 7537 4 (ebook)

British Library Cataloguing in Publication Data.
A catalogue record for this book is available from the British Library.

Origination by Amberley Publishing.
Printed in Great Britain.

Contents

Introduction

Manchester's story from an early Roman fort to a great metropolis is told through the treasure trove of images from the collection of Historic England.

The Roman fort at Castlefield, Mamucium or Mancunium, was constructed to protect the routes from Chester to York, south-west through Derby to London and north to Lancaster and Carlisle. The earliest settlement outside the fort (the vicus) was shown on early maps as Alport (old town).

By AD 923 the town had come under the rule of West Saxon kings. The historic centre of Manchester was now at the confluence of the River Irk and River Irwell. This was the site of the manor house of the Grelley family, and probably also their castle, which was recorded in 1184 – probably an earth and timber construction.

In 1086, when the Domesday Book was surveyed, Manchester was in the Salford hundred and was not granted a charter until 1301.

There is very little early ecclesiastical architecture. Manchester lacked extensive monastic land and so the city cannot claim an early abbey or priory. Manchester Cathedral, founded as a collegiate church in 1421, stands alone as an example of early church architecture in the city.

The Old Wellington Inn in Exchange Square is the best example of a timber-framed building from Manchester's post-medieval period. Built in 1552 next to the market square, it is in an area known as The Shambles. It was relocated after the IRA bombing to its current position by the cathedral.

Alport Lodge, owned by the Derby family, was destroyed in the Civil War. Many of the old halls were demolished without sentiment. The moated Radcliffe Hall was demolished in 1811. The hall stood on Pool Fold behind what is now Cross Street. Hulme Hall, which overlooked the River Irwell, was demolished in 1840. Ancoats Hall, built in 1609 by Oswald Mosley, was lost to the city in the 1960s.

The important medieval hall sites that remain are Clayton Hall, Wythenshawe Hall and Baguley Hall, which has been surveyed in detail. In Queen Anne's time many fine private houses appeared, such as Mr Dickenson's on Market Street. It was here that Bonnie Prince Charlie lodged during the Jacobite Rebellion in 1745 after his arrival in Manchester.

The eighteenth century was to present Manchester with the glorious Saint Ann's Church founded by Lady Ann Bland (née Mosley). St John's Street remains from the Georgian period but many fine terraces were sadly destroyed in the Manchester Blitz.

In the earlier half of the 1800s Greek revival style was fashionable and examples of this are the Portico Library, the Athenaeum, the Bank of England on King Street and the Theatre Royal in Peter Street. Later, the architects of the nineteenth century favoured the Gothic style: the Town Hall, John Rylands Library, the Assize Courts and Owen's College are all examples of this.

From any tall building in the centre of Manchester you can see the Pennines to the north and east. It is said that this position, giving Manchester its damp climate and constant water supply from the many rivers that flowed down from

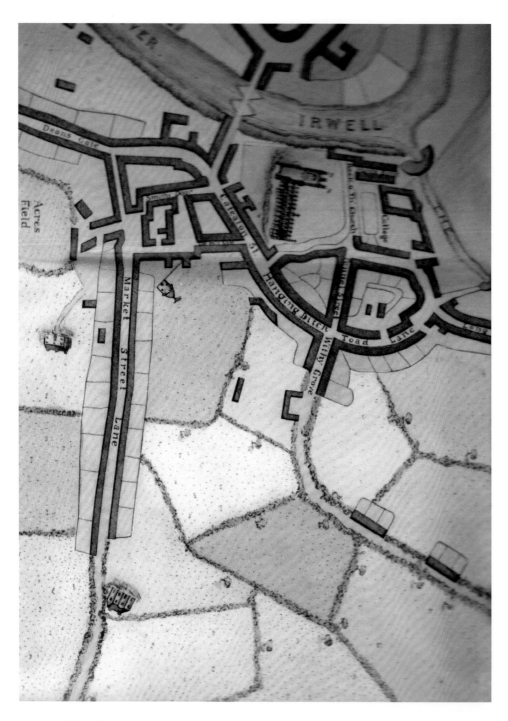

A map of Manchester, 1665.

the Pennines, was instrumental in making Manchester the cotton capital of the world. The climate may have been helpful but it was the new transport links that transformed Manchester: the Bridgewater Canal, the Rochdale Canal, the oldest standing passenger railway station in the world and, of course, the Manchester Ship Canal.

The textile industry gives Manchester its unique Victorian appearance. The red-brick buildings, built in monumental style, give the city its distinctive character and reflects Manchester's history as the 'Cottonopolis'. The impressive commercial warehouses, often built in the palazzo style, were designed to demonstrate the great wealth of Manchester's cotton merchants and to act as vast wholesale showrooms.

Manchester was not only at the centre of the cotton industry but it was also at the centre of many innovations such as Joseph Whitworth's standardised screw threads, James Nasmyth's steam hammer, John Dalton developing modern atomic theory, Rutherford splitting the atom in 1913 and Alan Turing and colleagues developing the world's first computer in 1948.

At the opening of the twentieth century Manchester was reaping the benefits of one of the most ambitious municipal undertakings of the nineteenth century, the Manchester Ship Canal, which opened in 1894. Its success is reflected in the proliferation of commercial buildings of the early twentieth century, among the most significant of which are Bridgewater House, India House and Lancaster House on Whitworth Street.

After the First World War the major civic undertaking in the centre was the Central Library and Town Hall extension by Vincent Harris, built between 1930 and 1938.

The best of all the 1960s buildings is the group of Co-operative Insurance Society and Co-operative Wholesale Society buildings on Miller Street. New buildings of the 1970s were less ambitious. Although the high-tech Royal Exchange Theatre pod of 1976 is a successful example of creativity, the period is memorable mainly for the erection of the inward-looking Arndale Centre.

The twenty-first century has seen some fine new buildings. The Beetham Tower is a landmark forty-seven-storey mixed-use skyscraper, and was designed by Simpson, Haugh & Partners. Urbis was an exhibition and museum designed by Ian Simpson. The building opened in June 2002 as part of the redevelopment of Exchange Square known as the Millennium Quarter, and is now the National Football Museum. The Manchester skyline is again being transformed and taller modern buildings now sit side by side with the Victorian buildings.

The Town Hall, 1877
This magnificent Gothic building was built to replace the earlier Town Hall on the corner of King Street and Cross Street. Designed by Alfred Waterhouse and built in 1868–77, it was constructed to reflect Manchester's wealth and importance in the Victorian age. The building cost £859,000 in total. It was to be equal, if not superior, to any similar building in the country and the funding was to reflect this. Waterhouse won the design competition and produced a building of great subtlety and refinement. Pevsner stated, 'The building stands as one of the greatest and most original architectural works of Victorian England'.

The Town Hall Interior, 1877
The plan of the Town Hall is a hollow triangle with fine state apartments on the first floor overlooking Albert Square. These rooms are the Banqueting room, Reception room, the Mayor's Parlour and the Council Chamber, which was designed to seat forty-eight aldermen and councillors. The Great Hall stands in the centre and each corner has a fine circular staircase, incorporating an open well, so that warm air can rise up from a basement boiler. The richness of the architecture has made it an ideal location for film makers to use it to represent the Palace of Westminster.

Manchester Cathedral, 1973

Manchester Cathedral is an impressive late medieval collegiate church and consists chiefly of late Perpendicular English architecture. The present building dates from around 1421, when Thomas De La Warre obtained a licence from Henry V for a collegiate foundation. Dedicated to St Mary, St Denys and St George, it became a cathedral in 1847. Despite many restorations the church has managed to preserve much evidence of its architectural history. Carvings on the misericords are exceptional and considered to be among the finest in Europe. They depict medieval tales and legends. In the fifteenth century the church began to be enlarged by the addition of chantry chapels. The new north porch was added in 1889 to replace the original medieval one. In 1940 a German bomb destroyed most of the north-east of the cathedral and caused extensive damage to the rest of the building. The damage was so severe that there were thoughts that it could not be repaired. In the end the reconstruction took twenty years to complete.

THE CLOISTERS CHETHAM HOSPITAL MANCHESTER

Chetham's, 1900

Chetham's was originally built around 1421 as the domestic premises of the priests' college attached to the collegiate church. They are the best preserved buildings of their type and date in the country. In 1653 the wealthy merchant Sir Humphrey Chetham left instructions in his will for the buildings to become a charity school or 'hospital' and library. This resulted in a wonderful medieval building being saved for Manchester. Chetham's library has been in continuous use as a free public library for over 350 years. It was the setting for Engels when he was researching *The Condition of the Working Class in England*, and it was here that he formed his lifelong friendship with Karl Marx.

St Ann's Church, 1912
Lady Ann Bland nee Mosley laid the foundation stone of St Ann's Church in 1709. She was prompted by a desire to create an alternative to the collegiate church. The church influenced the local architectural style of the city. It is a neoclassical building, originally constructed from locally quarried, red Collyhurst sandstone, although, due to its soft nature, some of the original stone has since been replaced with sandstone of various colours. The church has features reminiscent of St Paul's Cathedral and has been attributed to Sir Christopher Wren. The church was sensitively restored and remodelled by Alfred Waterhouse in 1887.

St. Ann's Square, Manchester.

Above: Central Library, 1934

The design of the Central Library was again chosen by competition. Won by Vincent Harris, it was built between 1930 and 1934. Its Roman imperial design is a huge success. Its five-bay porticos of Corinthian columns provide a landmark entrance to the city from the south. Opened by George V in July 1934, it has recently been transformed to meet the needs of the twenty-first century. Since its opening the library entrance has been a favourite meeting point for Mancunians. The elevated view above shows the Central Library during its construction.

Opposite above and below: Town Hall Extension, 1938

The Town Hall extension was also designed by Vincent Harris to complement the new library. It was built to provide additional accommodation for local government services. It is perhaps not a successful as the library, and has been described by some as dull and drab, but also as Harris's 'best job' by Pevsner. The building is boosted by an usual skyline and has a more traditional neo-Georgian character where it faces the library. The anteroom in the extension building is much admired: 'First you notice the light streaming in from the four huge windows, which give it an Elizabethan Long Gallery feel, such as you might find in Haddon Hall or Lyme Park.'

CENOTAPH, ST. PETER'S SQUARE, MANCHESTER. No.2.

The Cenotaph, St Peter's Square, 1931
The buildings in the background were all demolished to make way for the Central Library and Town Hall extension. The Peace Garden was developed in 1999 with a children's play area and peace pagoda. In 2015 the space was remodelled to make way for the Metro link trams and the cenotaph was repositioned.

Above: Mechanics' Institute, 2000

The world's first mechanics' institute was established in Edinburgh in 1821. The movement worked to provide technical education for working people and a free library. With Manchester's radical history, it was not surprising that it was one of the earliest to be built. It was established in 1824 at the Bridgewater Arms Hotel by a group of wealthy manufacturers and scientists. The inaugural meeting of the Trades Union Congress was held here in 1868. In 1882 it was decided to establish a technical school, the Technical School and Mechanics' Institution, which opened in September 1855. This was the beginning of the institution later known as UMIST. The building now contains archives from the National Labour Museum.

Opposite above and below: The Athenaeum, Princess Street, 1870–1920

The Athenaeum is now part of Manchester Art Gallery and linked to the gallery by a glass atrium. It was built for a Manchester society for the 'advancement and diffusion of knowledge'. Sir Charles Barry designed the building in the Italian palazzo style, among the first of such buildings in the city, in 1837. Richard Cobden was instrumental in promoting education in the city and spoke at the opening, and within four years it had over 1,000 members. Charles Dickens and Benjamin Disraeli addressed its membership in the 1840s. The club declined after 1935.

Manchester Royal Infirmary, Piccadilly, *c.* 1900

The hospital was founded in 1752 by Charles White, a Manchester doctor, and the local merchant Joseph Bancroft. Charles White studied medicine in London and Edinburgh. His speciality was obstetrics, where his modern practices earned him an international reputation. His work resulted in a massive drop in the rate of infant mortality. The original twelve-bed hospital building was in a house on Garden Street in Shudehill, but it was soon apparent that a larger hospital was required. The Lord of the Manor, Sir Oswald Mosely, donated land at the top of Market Street (now known as Piccadilly Gardens) and a fine new hospital was opened in 1775. The hospital grew in size over the years to accommodate a psychiatric hospital, public baths and outpatient's department. In 1908 the new infirmary was opened in Oxford Road and this building was demolished to make way for Piccadilly Gardens.

Central Police and Fire Station, London Road, 1986

The competition to design the building was judged by Alfred Waterhouse and was built by Woodhouse, Willoughby & Langham in 1901–06, and is characteristic of many of Manchester's buildings of the time. The style is neo-baroque and is built in red brick and terracotta. It was magnificent headquarters for the fire service, providing accommodation for the fire officers and their families. It closed in 1986 and plans to convert it into a boutique hotel are now being explored.

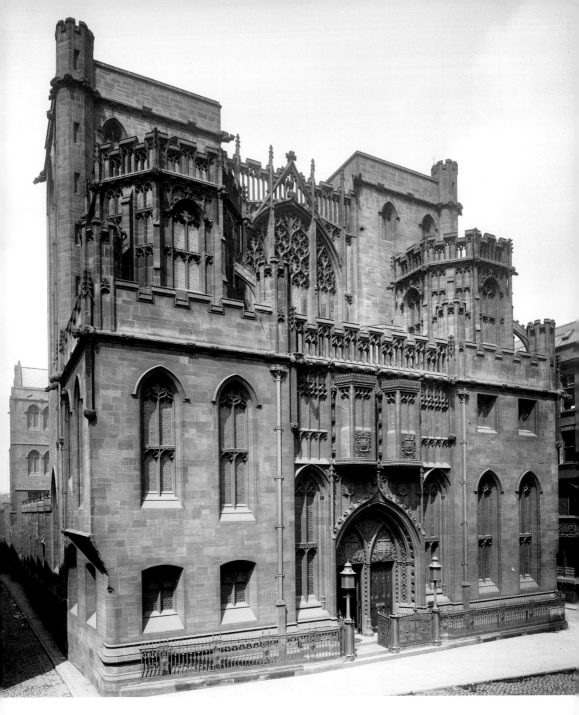

John Rylands Library, Deansgate, 1900

John Rylands Library was erected by his widow Enriqueta as a permanent memorial to her beloved husband. In 1890 she appointed Basil Champney as the architect. No expense was to be spared. It cost £230,000 and was not finished until 1899. The library was inaugurated on 6 October 1899, when Mrs Rylands received the Freedom of the City of Manchester. As the building would contain valuable manuscripts, Enriqueta insisted that the roof should not be combustible. It is built in red sandstone. She purchased the famous Althorp library from Lord Spencer in 1892, and continued to add priceless additions to the library.

Statue of John Rylands, 1900

This full-sized marble statue of John Rylands is by John Cassidy and stands in the historic reading room. His invoice shows it cost £1,325. John Rylands was born in St Helens in 1888 and his family were cotton manufacturers. He quickly became the owner of the largest textile manufacturing concern in the United Kingdom, and Manchester's first multimillionaire. His fine warehouse built in Market Street can still be seen today as a Debenhams store. The building was designed in an art deco style and is clad in Portland stone.

Commerce

Bank of England, 1898
The Bank of England lost its monopoly of joint stock banking rights in 1833 and as compensation was allowed to build banks in the provinces. Charles Robert Cockerell was asked to produce designs for branches in Manchester, Liverpool and Bristol, of which the Manchester branch is the earliest (1845–46) and possibly the finest. King Street was always an important street and quickly became a centre for the banking trade.

The Refuge Building, 1912
A major landmark on Oxford
Street, the Refuge Building was
built for the assurance company
on the corner of Whitworth Street.
Designed by Alfred Waterhouse,
building began in 1891, and has
been added to over the years.
The decoration is in the northern
Italian style. As we can see the
interior is equally impressive.
In 1996, it was converted into
The Palace Hotel and has now
been transformed again into a
spectacular hotel – The Principle.

The Tootal Building, 1900
The Tootal building was designed
by Joseph Gibbons Sankey in the
neo-baroque style in 1896. Angular
towers topped by lanterns stand at the
corners of this red-brick and terracotta
structure. Along the Oxford Street
side, giant Corinthian columns divide
the bays. On the canal side a similar
pattern continues, this time with
pilasters.

  The interior has now been
redesigned, but a First World War
memorial by Henry Sellers has been
retained. We also see the clerks'
office. Sir Edward Tootal Broadhurst
was a director and eventually
chairman of Tootal Broadhurst
Lee, one of the largest cotton
manufacturers in Manchester.

St James's Buildings, 1912
The headquarters of Calico Printer's Association, this fine building was built in 1912, again illustrating the importance of Manchester as the headquarters of the textile trade in Britain. The Calico Printers' Association Ltd was a British textile company founded in 1899, from the amalgamation of forty-six textile printing companies and thirteen textile merchants. The industry prospered in the latter half of the nineteenth century. The company at its inception accounted for over 80 per cent of Britain's output of printed cloth. Pevsner considers the entrance hall to be the most opulent of the surviving Manchester warehouses.

Sunlight House, Quay Street, 1958
The headquarters of Joseph Sunlight's property business, Sunlight House was originally intended to be thirty storeys high. Built in 1932, it is constructed of steel and concrete and clad in Portland stone. The building is square in plan with a central light well and is fourteen storeys high including the attic storeys. It has an eight-bay façade and a wide canted corner to the right-hand side, which rises to an octagonal turret and terminates in a domed lantern with an apex finial. On completion, it was the city's tallest building. Its art deco design, complete with mansard roofs, make the building a distinctive feature in the city. In the basement there is a fine original swimming pool.

Hudson Building, Great Ancoats Street, 2008
The Hudson building is a fine example of well-crafted art deco architecture. Constructed in 1924, this former warehouse has huge Crittall-style windows and a beautifully ornate façade. Crittall Windows is a notable English manufacturer of steel-framed windows. They are particularly associated with the art deco and modernist movements in early twentieth-century architecture. The building has now been converted into attractive residential apartments. To the left we see the Methodist Women's Night Shelter, which opened in 1899.

Co-operative Insurance Society Building, Miller Street, 2000
This area is dominated by the Co-operative group. An office skyscraper, completed in 1962 and raising to 387 feet in height, it was designed by G. S. Hay and Gordon Tait. It has a strikingly elegant and sophisticated design inspired by Skidmore, Owings & Merrill's Inland Steel building in Chicago. With its imposing scale and massing, it is highly successful in conveying the status and prestige of the CIS and the wider Co-operative movement, and the strength of the financial community within Manchester.

New Century House, 2007
A sister building to the CIS Tower, this attached hall, New Century Hall, has a capacity of 1,000 people. New Century House and Hall were listed in 1995 as Grade II and is a good example of a high-quality post-war office building. It is considered one of the finest later twentieth-century towers in the United Kingdom alongside the sister building CIS Tower. The twenty-first-century expression of the Co-op group can be seen in the striking No. 1 Angel Square, a landmark building. It was completed in 2013, standing 72.5 metres. The building forms the centrepiece of the new £800-million NOMA development in the Angel Meadow area.

Canada House, 2001
Canada House is an office building on
Chepstow Street. Constructed originally
as a warehouse, the building opened
in 1909. Designed by local architect
W. & G. Higginbottom, the building has
features consistent with the art nouveau
style and a terracotta exterior. Each floor
was served by full hydraulic goods hoists.

Lancashire & Yorkshire Bank, 1890
The bank stands proudly at the top
of King Street. Built around 1888 and
designed by Heathcote and Rawle, it
is in a Free Renaissance style. It's huge
and splendid banking hall contains twin
saucer domes, polished granite columns
and marble-lined walls. This can still
be seen today as it is now an Italian
restaurant – Rosso's.

Music and Theatre

The Free Trade Hall, 1957
Designed by Edward Walters and completed in 1856, this great hall represents Manchester's radical history as a centre for the free trade movement. It was built to house the gatherings of the Anti-Corn Law League. The land was given by Richard Cobden, a great champion of free trade. It was on this site in Petersfield that the infamous Peterloo Massacre occurred in 1819. Eleven people were reported killed and 140 injured when the yeomanry charged the crowd.

The Free Trade Hall, Front Arcade, 2000
Built in fine Yorkshire sandstone, the façade is classically orthodox consisting of nine bays in the Renaissance style. The hall became the home of the Hallé Orchestra. The hall was bombed in the Manchester Blitz and a new hall was constructed in 1951 behind two walls of the original façade. Mancunians will also remember the hall as the venue for school prize-giving celebrations.

The Free Trade Hall Artists' Signatures, 2001

Hallé was born Karl Hallé in Germany in 1819. After settling in England, he changed his name to Charles Hallé. He moved to Manchester in 1853 and formed the Hallé Orchestra. The orchestra went through good times and bad but has remained one of the country's leading orchestras. This photograph of artist's signatures in a dressing room reflects the quality of the visiting musicians. At the bottom left-hand corner we see the signature of Yehudi Menuhin, who was in Manchester to perform Bartok's violin concerto, Elgar's violin concerto and Beethoven's *Eroica*.

Bridgewater Hall, 2011

Proposals to replace the Free Trade Hall had existed since it was damaged in the Second World War. Despite being a popular venue, the acoustics were poor. The Bridgewater Hall held its first concert in September 1996 and was officially opened on 4 December by Elizabeth II accompanied by the Duke of Edinburgh. The new hall was one of a number of structures built in the 1990s that symbolised the transition to a new and modern Manchester. This fine auditorium is set at an angle to Barbirolli Square and has a bold prow pointing towards St Peter's Square. It is considered a great success. Built by the side of the Rochdale Canal, there are fine views from the interior of the canal and the red-brick warehouses.

Warehouse Lower Mosley Street

The People's Concert Hall, or Cass, *c.* 1875
The People's Concert Hall stood on the site of the Midland Hotel in Lower Mosley Street. Originally a warehouse, by 1853 it was 'The Casino' and was later known as the People's Concert Hall, providing entertainment for the working classes. Sadly its reputation became rather tainted before its demolition, as it became the favourite venue for working-class gangs of the city.

The Comedy Theatre, Peter Street, 1885
The Comedy Theatre opened for business in 1884. The architect was Alfred Derbyshire, a pupil of Richard Lane, who designed the nearby Friends' Meeting House. In 1908 the theatre was sold to Annie Horniman, who bought it for £25,000 and commissioned Frank Matcham to redesign it. It reopened in 1912 as the Gaiety Theatre with a reduced capacity of 1,300. It became famous as Britain's first regional repertory theatre.

The Palace Theatre, Oxford Street, 1875–1900
Designed by Alfred Darbyshire in 1891 at a cost of £40,500, the first production at the Palace Theatre was the ballet *Cleopatra*. The interior of the theatre was renovated by Bertie Crewe in 1913, which took seven months. The theatre reopened with a reduced seating capacity of 2,600. Until the First World War the theatre was the home of the best variety in the city. In September 1940 it took a direct hit from a German bomb during the Manchester Blitz. The rebuilding was not a success. This beautiful building was covered in tile cladding in 1955.

New Theatre, Quay Street, 1913
The theatre opened as the New Theatre on
Boxing Day 1912. It was built in the classical
style by Richardson & Gill and Farquarson,
and over the entrance are three pairs of fluted
Ionic columns. The New Theatre struggled to
compete with other theatres in the city and in
1915 it was sold to United Theatre Ltd and
renamed the New Queen's Theatre. Sir Thomas
Beecham performed there on several occasions
and it was in honour of him that the theatre
was renamed the Opera House.

The Picture House, 1915

The building still stands on the corner of Oxford Street and Chepstow Street. Built in 1911 for the Provincial Cinematography Theatre Company, it was later called the Oxford Picture House. Naylor and Sale were the architects of what was one of the first purpose-built cinemas in the city centre. It is built of red brick with orange terracotta features. Apart from the tower, the upper façade remains intact, but at street level it has been transformed into a modern retail development.

Streets

Piccadilly, 1903
A view looking towards the Royal Hotel, showing the street crowded with pedestrians, trams and horse-drawn traffic. The Royal Hotel stood on the corner of Market Street and Mosley Street. It was here in 1888 that the first professional football league was formally created. The Royal Hotel was demolished to make way for an extension to Lewis's store in 1908.

Piccadilly 1903
The statue of Arthur Wellesley, Duke of Wellington, stands in the foreground. The statue, designed by Matthew Noble, is much larger than life-size. It shows him in later life, speaking in the House of Lords, with his military despatches at his feet and dressed in a frock coat with military decorations. The monument was a controversial one, partly because public opinion favoured an equestrian statue.

Piccadilly Gardens, 1910–40

Before 1755 the area, which originally was occupied by water-filled clay pits, was called the Daub Holes. The Lord of the Manor donated the site and the pits were replaced by a fine ornamental pond. The sunken gardens were established after the Manchester Royal Infirmary had been demolished. The gardens were redeveloped in 2001 and there are now plans to remove the controversial concrete wall, upgrade the grassed area and lighting, plant more trees, boost maintenance and open a new row of restaurants to replace the wall.

Deansgate, 1884

A view from near the junction with John Dalton Street, showing a man in the foreground riding a penny-farthing. Deansgate has always been a significant street in Manchester's history. If you follow the thoroughfare you are passing from the Roman fort at Castlefield to the centre of medieval Manchester and the site of the cathedral. It has become, along with King Street, one of the leading fashionable shopping areas of the town.

Deansgate Arcade, 1900
The Barton building was
designed by Corbett,
Raby & Sawyer and built
in 1871. Behind the façade
is a stunning glass-and-iron
shopping arcade. Pevsner
says that 'it is probably the
best example of cast iron and
glass roofed arcade anywhere
in the country'. Believed to
be influenced by the Galleria
Vittorio Emanuele in Milan,
everything is light and airy
with three tiers of balconies.
It is a Manchester treasure.

S. J. Waring & Sons,
Deansgate, 1897
In 1835 John Waring arrived
in Liverpool from Belfast
and established a wholesale
cabinet-making business in
Liverpool. He was succeeded
by his son Samuel James
Waring, also a cabinet maker.
The family business prospered
and in 1897 Waring and
Gillow was formed by the
merger of Gillow of Lancaster
with Waring of Liverpool.
This store on Deansgate was
for many years the furnishers
of choice for the wealthy
of Manchester.

Albert Square, 1903
The square, named after Prince Albert, was laid out to provide a space for the memorial
in 1864–67. It features a marble statue of Albert standing on a plinth and facing west,
designed by Matthew Noble. The figure is placed within a large medieval-style ciborium,
which was designed by the architect Thomas Worthington. Noble was commissioned by
Mayor Thomas Goadsby to sculpt the prince's likeness, and the designs were personally
approved by Queen Victoria. Clearing the site began in 1864, and required the demolition of
over 100 buildings, including the Engraver's Arms pub, a coffee-roasting works, a smithy, a
coal yard and various warehouses.

Market Buildings, Thomas Street, 2006
The first market stalls started to appear on Shudehill around 1844, and in 1900 Smithfield was the largest covered market in Britain. The former market offices were designed in 1877 by Travis and Mangnall, and built in red brick with stone dressings and fine first-floor windows. At the height of its success the market buildings dominated this area of the city. The area, now known as the Northern Quarter, is a thriving social area.

Wholesale Fish Market Detail, 2006
The Wholesale Fish Market was designed by Speakman, Son and Hickson in the Italianate Romanesque style. The market opened in 1873 and incorporated the latest features including large cellars and ice stores. This exterior view of the upper part of one of the end walls shows fine sculptures, by Joseph Bonehill, of fishermen at sea, landing their catch and selling it on. Some of the fine ironwork gates survive.

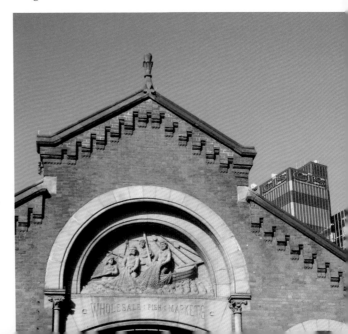

Hotels and Inns

Palm Court, Midland Hotel, 1912
Opened in September 1903, it was built by the Midland Railway to serve Manchester Central railway station. Designed by Charles Trubshaw in a highly individual Edwardian baroque style, it is clad in red brick, brown terracotta and several varieties of polished granite to withstand the polluted environment of Manchester. Always an important venue, it was here in the Palm Court that in 1904 Charles Rolls met Henry Royce leading to the formation of Rolls-Royce in 1904.

Albion Hotel, 1898
The hotel was on the corner of Piccadilly and Oldham Street. Although not as prestigious as the Midland Hotel, its fine restaurant was the venue for an historic meeting of journalists in 1906, which resulted in the National Union of Journalists. The hotel was demolished to make way for the new Woolworth's store in 1928.

Old Wellington Inn, 1971

This fine half-timbered pub is the oldest building of its kind in Manchester. It dates to the seventeenth century and was built next to the market square in an area known as The Shambles. It was purchased in 1554 by the Byrom family and became part-residence and part-drapers' shop. The premises were licensed in 1862 and became the Vintners Arms, then the Kenyon Vaults and later the Old Wellington Inn. This photograph shows the extensive building work in 1971 when the Arndale shopping centre was built. After the IRA bomb an ambitious plan was formed to move the building as Manchester could ill afford to lose one of its oldest buildings. This feat of engineering was a great success and it now stands close to Manchester Cathedral.

The Mosley Hotel, 1899

The Mosley Hotel occupied a prominent position on Piccadilly. It formed part of a block of buildings that was bounded by Tib Street, Back Piccadilly, Oldham Street and Piccadilly. The hotel was one of the busiest coaching inns until the coming of the railways and coaches ceased to run in 1833. The hotel, however, continued to flourish and was considered one of the four best hotels in Manchester and a rival to the Midland, as the fine interior drawing room illustrates.

The Britannia Hotel, 2000

The Britannia Hotel opened in 1858 as a textile warehouse for the wholesale drapery business of S. & J. Watts, and was designed by Travis and Mangnall. This was the largest wholesale drapery business in the city. When the elaborate Watts' Warehouse was begun in 1851, there were seven warehouses on Portland Street and four more were opened before it was finished. The square mile of 'Warehouse City' has been described as the finest example of a Victorian commercial centre in the United Kingdom.

Britannia Hotel Interior, 2000
The grand palazzo-style warehouses with their tall floor to ceiling heights and large areas of glazing have proved attractive for offices, hotels and residential use. Today it is the Britannia Hotel, opened in 1982, and as you can see, it still has its original, spectacular interior staircase, which has been lovingly restored.

Transport

Liverpool Road Station, 1998
Liverpool Road station is one of the most important railway stations in Britain, and the oldest surviving passenger railway station in the world. Manchester is said to have been the place where the railway age began. It was the service established between Liverpool and Manchester that first demonstrated the feasibility of rail as a viable transport system. Opened to the public in 1830, it marked the terminus of the newly created line, which ran from Liverpool to Manchester. It has been suggested that Liverpool Road station was designed by architect John Foster Jr (1786–1846.)

The Museum of Science and Industry, 1989
The Museum of Science and Industry now occupies the station site. It was opened on 15 September 1983 and later expanded to include the whole of the historic Liverpool Road station. The museum exhibits a large collection of stationary steam engines, hot air engines, diesel engines, hydraulic pumps, and large electric generators. Most of these machines are operational and can often be seen running.

Victoria Station, Manchester.

MHR. 26

Victoria Station, 1967–68
The station was opened in 1844 by the
Liverpool & Manchester Railway and
designed by Robert Stephenson in the
Italianate style. The long stone baroque
elevation is described by Pevsner as
unexciting. However, the attractive
canopy showing the destinations
is appealing. Queen Victoria gave
permission for the station to be
named after her. It was later enlarged
and soon became one of the largest
passenger stations in Britain.

Lancashire & Yorkshire War Memorial, 2000
This bronze war memorial was unveiled in 1922 by Field Marshall Haig. The huge ceramic map above, which probably dates from the time of rebuilding in 1904, shows the routes of the Lancashire & Yorkshire Railway system. L&YR operated most of the trains from the station between 1847 and 1923, when it became one of the main constituents of the London, Midland & Scottish Railway.

Lancashire & Yorkshire Railway Warehouse, Oldham Road, 1900–22
The goods station began life as a passenger station in 1839, but after the decision to build Victoria station, it was closed to passengers from 1844 and was transformed into a goods terminus. The station took a huge site between Rochdale Road and Oldham Road. The line came into the station by way of a viaduct that stood 30 feet above the surrounding streets. It is said that 'a flight of spacious stairs was used by passengers to reach the very commodious station building'.

Oldham Road Goods Station, Ancoats, 1927

After the transfer of passenger traffic to Victoria, the site became a huge transport depot. An elaborate system of lifts and turntables facilitated the unloading and loading of goods. A number of warehouses were built on the site dedicated to the storage of a variety of products including fruit, fish, cloth, grain and potatoes. Here we see employees processing bananas in the depot of John Swift, fruit merchant, the Rowntree's depot and Fry's vans outside the grain warehouse. The station closed in 1968 and there is little evidence left that it was once such a busy hub.

Oxford Road Station, 1997
The station was opened on 20 July 1849 by the Manchester, South Junction & Altrincham Railway, and until 1904 was their headquarters. Pevsner describes the station as 'One of the most remarkable and unusual stations in the country both for the architectural form and the technological interest … it is the most dramatic and it is an important example of the deployment of timber to achieve large roof spans incorporating clerestory lighting.' The elegant 1960s design we see today is by British Railways architect Max Clendinning, and the engineer was Hugh Tottenham.

Public Parks

Whitworth Institute, Whitworth Park, Manchester

Whitworth Institute, 1910–40
Manchester has Sir Joseph Whitworth to thank for this park and gallery. He is best known for his standardisation of screw threads known as British Standard Whitworth. After his death his fortune was used to finance public works. The Whitworth Institute was established in 1888 in Grove House, to accommodate a growing collection of sculpture and paintings. In 1891 an architectural competition to rebuild Grove House as an art gallery was won by J. W. Beaumont, a Manchester architect. The rear part of Grove House was demolished to make way for new galleries built to the winning design between 1892 and 1898. The gallery is still flourishing. It was completely refurbished in 2015 providing more space for displaying the 55,000 items in the gallery's collection. The Whitworth won the Museum of the Year award in 2015.

WHITWORTH PARK MANCHESTER

Whitworth Park, 1904–09
Joseph Whitworth's bequest funded both the art gallery and the park. It was his executor, Robert Dukinfield Darbishire, who ensured his plans came to fruition. He sent Alfred Wilsher, park superintendent, to the Continent to see examples and the gardens on Potters Field were relaid to produce a fine park with wide avenues, new trees and flower beds, a bandstand and shelters. A lake was added later with a large fountain, islands, boathouse and pavilion. The park was leased to the Corporation of Manchester by the Whitworth Trustees in October 1904.

Lake in Whitworth Park, Manchester

Heaton Hall, 1902

In 1772 Sir Thomas Egerton commissioned the design of his new home in the park for himself and his new wife. Being young and wealthy, Sir Thomas employed the one of the best, most fashionable architects of the time – James Wyatt. Heaton Hall, and the other magnificent buildings that Wyatt and his family designed, can still be seen around the park. The entrance into the house is on the north side and has a restrained frontage, with the main façade and the main rooms on the south side.

Boggart Hole Clough, 1900–30
Boggart Hole Clough is an old deer park owned by the Lord of the Manor. The park was
the venue for mass meetings. In 1896 Emmeline Pankhurst and Keir Hardie addressed an
Independent Labour Party meeting of up to 50,000. In 1911 the area was purchased by
Manchester Corporation and gradually transformed into a magnificent country park, boating
lake, running tracks, cafés and open-air theatre. On Sunday afternoons the park rang out to the
sound of brass band concerts. The clough was famed for its peacocks. The broad walk was laid
out by the Corporation in the early 1900s. It still retains its elegance today.

The Broad Walk. Boggart Hole Clough

Above: Alexandra Park, 1910–20

Alexandra Park was designed in 1869 by Alexander Hennell, opened to the public in 1870 and named for Princess Alexandra, the wife of Queen Victoria's son Edward. Hennell's design was experimental in its use of oval shaped and curved pathways, which contrasted with the more rigid geometry seen previously in some Victorian landscapes. The lodge and gateways are the work of Alfred Darbyshire. Its initial purpose was to 'deter the working men of Manchester from the alehouses during their day off'. The park has just been restored to its former glory.

Below: Philips Park, 1900–30

One of the first municipal parks in the country, Philips Park dates back to 1846 and is one of the largest parks in Greater Manchester. It is named after the Manchester MP Mark Philips, who promoted the need for public parks in Manchester. It was designed by Joshua Major following an open competition and opened in 1846. This historic park is Grade II listed and many of its original features remain to this day, including the carriage drive, serpentine paths, amphitheatre and the head gardener's house. The park has undergone notable refurbishment, and today is a key green space within the Medlock River Valley corridor.

Above: Castlefield, 1998

Castlefield is the site of the Roman settlement of AD 79 – Mancunium, the birthplace of Manchester. In 1765 the Bridgewater Canal was opened at Castlefield, creating a level link by water between the Duke of Bridgewater's coal mines at Worsley and the centre of Manchester. The area has been landscaped retaining the names of the great warehouses built around this basin. Many are still standing and have been converted for modern use. We see a general view of the Merchant's Bridge in the Castlefield Basin.

Opposite above and below: Victoria Baths, 1993

When it opened in 1906, the building was described as 'the most splendid municipal bathing institution in the country' and 'a water palace of which every citizen of Manchester can be proud'. Not only did the building provide spacious and extensive facilities for swimming, bathing and leisure, it was built of the highest quality materials with many period decorative features, including stained glass, terracotta, tiles and mosaic floors. When Manchester City Council decided it had to close Victoria Baths in 1993, there was a vigorous reaction in the local community. Manchester residents greatly valued the Turkish baths, the Aeratone bath, the swimming facilities, and the building itself. After considerable work the building is now partially restored and volunteers continue to work towards full restoration.

Above: Merchants Warehouse, 2000
The warehouse was completed in 1827. It is an architectural triumph and is the oldest surviving warehouse on the canal. The warehouse takes its name from the main tenant – The Merchants Company. It was destroyed by fire in 1829 and was rebuilt in 1830. Boats would enter through the arches and hoists would load and offload goods. In the 1970s it was once more badly damaged by fire. Ian Simpson Architects completely restored the building between 1995 and 1997.

Below: The Rochdale Canal, 2011
The Rochdale Canal flows from Manchester to Sowerby Bridge where it joins with the Calder & Hebble Navigation. The Duke of Bridgewater had at first refused permission to allow the proposed canal to join onto the Bridgewater Canal, meaning the canal would terminate at Piccadilly. The canal eventually opened through to Manchester in 1804. This general view looking east shows the Rochdale Canal at Tib Lock.

Mills

McConnel & Kennedy Mills, 2000

Ancoats contains many historic cotton spinning mills. The development of the canal network was a vitally important factor in the development of Ancoats – 'one of the most intensely developed industrial centres in the world of its time' (Pevsner) – allowing transport of raw materials and finished goods, as well as providing water for the steam engines powering the mills and factories. McConnel & Kennedy Mills are on Redhill Street beside the Rochdale Canal. James McConnel and John Kennedy came from Scotland and set up the company in 1791.

Murray Mills, 2001
Adam and George Murray developed their mills beside the canal in competition with McConnel & Kennedy. This became the largest mill complex in the town. The buildings are arranged around a courtyard containing a canal basin now filled in and connected to the Rochdale Canal by tunnel. The remains of a detached engine house and chimney relate to improvements in 1870–80. Below is an interior view of Decker Mill showing a staggered line of columns.

Crime and Punishment

The Manchester Assize Court
In 1858 a competition was announced for the construction of a new assize court building to be erected on Great Ducie Street. Among the architects submitting drawings were Thomas Worthington and a twenty-nine-year-old Alfred Waterhouse. Waterhouse won the competition. The high-pitched roofs of the assize courts (and later the Town Hall and Owen's College) reflect his interest in the architecture of Antwerp and Bruges. Building began in 1859 and the first hearings took place in July of 1864. Even before the court house was finished, Waterhouse was commissioned to design the adjoining Strangeways Prison. Sadly the building was hit in the blitzes of 1940 and 1941 and was demolished.

Manchester Crown Court, Crown Square, 2012 Manchester Crown Court was built between 1957 and 1962 and designed by Leonard C. Howitt, the Manchester city architect. The courts of justice were built to replace the assize courts, which had been badly damaged during the war. It has a façade clad in Portland stone and features a ceremonial entrance with an elaborate canopy.

HMP Prison Manchester, 1996
The building was opened on 25 June 1868 to replace the New Bailey Prison in Salford. The distinctive building with its high minaret chimney is a famous landmark in the city. The architectural motifs are Romanesque. Waterhouse based his design on Joshua Jebb's plan for Pentonville Prison. The jail was built on the grounds of Strangeways Park and Gardens, from which it was named.

Greater Manchester Police Museum, 2005
Opened in 1981, the police museum is based in the Victorian police station on Newton Street.
Manchester Borough Police were founded in 1839. This former police station was built in 1879.
The museum contains the station's original charge office, cells and a Victorian magistrates'
court rescued from Denton Police Station, together with displays of uniforms and equipment
through the ages.

Victoria Park Housing

Crescent, Victoria Park, Manchester

The Crescent, Victoria Park, 1903–08
The park had its beginnings in a town-planning scheme, which was any early form of the planned residential suburb (laid out in one go according to Pevsner). It was built to provide new homes for wealthy residents away from dirty Manchester and was among the first gated suburban residential parks in England. The name was chosen in the reign of William IV in honour of the future Queen Victoria. Much of the land included in the park had belonged to John Dickenson. By 1850, sixty-five villas had been built in the park. Such was the prestige of a home in Victoria Park that in 1872 W. R. Callender MP entertained Disraeli at Ashburne House.

Regent House, Front View.

Regent House, 1872–77

A great example of one of the many fine villas built in the area. By the 1870s the property included a grand house, conservatories, stables and a fine planted garden, within a semi-rural setting. In the 1861 census, Julius Knoop and his wife Theodora are recorded as living at Regent House. He was a director of De Jersey and Co., merchants specialising in the export trade to Russia.

Housing

Above: Victoria Square, Ancoats, 2008
This is a very different housing scheme named for Victoria, with tenements designed by Spalding & Cross in 1889–97. It was the first example of municipal housing in the country and was built to provide better homes for the thousands of mill workers who had flooded into Ancoats. The image shows a five-storeyed block with an inner courtyard. The front elevation has some terracotta and Dutch side gables.

Opposite above and below: George Leigh Street School, 2008
The free school was built in 1912. So cramped were the schools surroundings when it was built that the playground was on the roof, hence the railings. The photograph below shows the building in George Leigh Street and Anita Street. The land had been owned by the Leigh family, giving the street its name. These houses were built to a high standard for working-class houses of the time. Pevsner says of them that they were three-bedroomed dwellings that 'conform to the moral idea for housing'.

St Peter's Church, Blossom Street 2001

By the time St Peter's was built in 1859, Ancoats had been transformed from a small township into a bustling and overcrowded industrial place. It was the first Anglican church to be built in this predominantly Roman Catholic community. The declining congregations resulted in its closure in 1960. This landmark Romanesque church is now restored and acts as a symbol of Ancoats growing regeneration from its former dereliction. In the image above we can see a sculpture group, part of a series called *The Peeps* by Dan Dubowitz. The church is now a permanent rehearsal centre for the Hallé ensembles and a resource for the whole community.

FAT Housing, 2011

Another unusual example of regeneration in Ancoats in Islington Square, New Islington, Ancoats. FAT were selected unanimously by the future residents to design twenty-three new houses for the Manchester Methodist Housing Group development by Urban Splash. The scheme comprises of twenty-three two- to four-bedroom family homes and garden areas. The scheme was developed in close collaboration with the residents. The striking houses are comfortable, functional and cosy with balconies, garages and gardens.

Chips Building, 2011

Chips building is a residential apartment building alongside the Ashton Canal in New Islington, and is an example of the regeneration of Victorian Ancoats, which has been led by Urban Splash. Designed by Will Allsop, the eight-storey building was conceived as 'three fat chips stacked on top of each other'. The building is clad in a composite wall faced with a cladding covered in newspaper print and text that echoes the industrial heritage of the Ancoats area. It has been described as 'quirky, bold and robust'.

Education

Above: Municipal School of Technology, 1902
The school building was begun in 1895 and completed in 1912, to designs by the architectural firm of Spalding and Cross. It has subsequently become part of the University of Manchester and renamed the Institute of Science and Technology. Pevsner states 'A splendid example of municipal pride and confidence' and 'built in the Loire Style with red sandstone and terracotta panels showing Renaissance motifs'.

Opposite: Renold Building, 2010
The Renold building opened in 1962 for the Manchester College of Science and Technology as part of a major expansion of its campus in the 1960s. The architect was W. A. Gibbon from the firm of Cruikshank and Seward. The foundation stone was laid on 24 June 1960 by Sir Charles Renold J. P. LLD (1883–1967), vice-president of the college, and chairman of the planning and development committee, after whom it was named. The building, which is made of concrete, consists of a two-storey base supporting a six-storey tower. There is a large glass-sided stair tower on the side. Inside is an impressive entrance hall on two levels with a large mural titled *Metamorphosis*, by Victor Pasmore in 1968.

Above: Clayton Hall, *c.* 1900

Clayton Hall is one of the earliest surviving buildings in Manchester and a rare example of a moated medieval site. The site was owned by the Clayton family and later the Byron family and may date from the twelfth century. It later became the home of Humphrey Chetham. In 1896 it was purchased by Manchester Corporation. The two-bay hall is timber framed and has a massive external chimney. It is one of a few examples in south-east Lancashire where a floor seems to be an insertion into an open hall. Clayton Hall is managed by the Friends of Clayton Park, who open the hall to the public and organise and run school and group visits.

Opposite: Charter Street Working Girls' Home, 2000

The original school was opened in 1847 but the present building was begun in 1866. In 1892 it was renamed as Charter Street Ragged School and Working Girls' Home. It is an early and remarkable example of a purpose-built ragged school. It provided food, clogs and clothing for children, and a Sunday breakfast for destitute men and women; medical services were also provided. The working girls' home was on the top floor with its own separate entrance on Dantzic Street. In July 1900 the school was visited by the Duchess of Sutherland, following a line of many dignitaries including Winston Churchill and General Booth.

Above and below: Baguley Hall, *c.* 1900
A classic example of a medieval H-plan house. It was built in the fourteenth century for Sir William De Baguley. The hall remained in the possession of the De Baguleys and later the Legh family of Knutsford. It is the best medieval secular building within the boundaries of the city, consisting of a timber-framed hall and two brick wings. It is unusual as the timbers are huge and are planks not posts or beams. The hall has tall mullioned windows of a later date. The doorway inside the gabled late sixteenth-century porch is original and so are the three doorways from the screens passage formerly leading to the kitchen, buttery and pantry. Two of them are blocked. Below is an interior view of Baguley Hall looking from the north into the hall through a timber-arched doorway.

Religion

Friends Meeting House, 2000

The Quakers have existed in Manchester since the time of George Fox, who visited the town in 1647, and again in 1657. The first Quaker meeting house to be built on the current site at Mount Street was built in 1795. The building seen today was completed in 1830 from the designs of Richard Lane, a Quaker architect, whose pupil was Alfred Waterhouse. The cost of the building, £7,600, was raised by subscription from local Quakers, one of whom was John Dalton, the famous chemist and discoverer of atomic theory, who worshipped here for many years.

Albert Memorial Hall, Peter Street, 1995

Albert Memorial Hal was built for for the Wesleyan Mission in 1908 and opened in 1910. The Methodists built many central halls in inner cities and this was one of the largest when it was built. Albert Hall was built by J. Gerrard & Sons of Swinton and designed in eclectic style with baroque and Gothic elements. The main hall on the first floor has a horseshoe gallery, sloping floor and coloured-glass roof lights. The finely detailed terracotta is formed into large windows at gallery level, and the interior is abundant in floral decoration in the plasterwork and glazed tiles. It is now sadly disused as a place of worship but is still used for concerts.

The New Synagogue, 2002

This is copy of an illustration of the synagogue often known as 'The Great Synagogue'. Designed by Thomas Bird, it opened on 14 March 1858 and closed in 1974. It was demolished in 1986. It was built in the Italian style with large Corinthian order columns and pilasters. It stood opposite the town hall and next to the fine library, dated 1876, on Cheetham Hill Road, which happily still stands today.

Reform Synagogue, Jacksons Row, 2002

Built in 1953 by Peter Cummings with Eric Levy, the movement for Reform Judaism is one of the oldest Reform synagogues. It was founded in Manchester in 1857. The current building was built in 1952, after the previous synagogue building was destroyed in 1941 during the Second World War in the Manchester Blitz. The building includes a large synagogue, banqueting hall and classrooms and sits at the heart of an area planned for redevelopment.

Above and below: The Jewish Museum, Cheetham Hill Road, 2000
These images shows the Spanish and Portuguese synagogue built in 1874 by Edward Salamons, a fine example of Victorian architecture, reflecting the Moorish style. It is built in red brick with stone dressings. The interior has been retained and has been lovingly preserved as the Manchester Jewish Museum, telling the story of Manchester Jewry.

Above: Manchester Central Mosque and Islamic Cultural Centre, Victoria Park, 2011
Sometimes referred to as Jamia Mosque, the Victoria Park mosque began as two adjacent houses. In 1971 the Jamiat-ul-Muslimeen commenced work on a purpose-built mosque; the two houses were demolished and the new look mosque took its current form, an individual design with a stepped tower topped by a gilded crescent. It was designed by Sir Frederick Gidderd, who also designed the Regents Park mosque.

Opposite above and below: Manchester Islamic Centre and Didsbury Mosque,
Burton Road, 2011
Originally the Albert Park Methodist chapel, it was built in 1883 in red brick with a corner spirelet. The chapel closed in 1962 and was later converted into a mosque. The interior view shows the mihrab niche in the mosque's prayer hall, and a pulpit retained from the building's previous use as a chapel.

About the Archive

Many of the images in this volume come from the Historic England Archive, which holds over 12 million photographs, drawings, plans and documents covering England's archaeology, architecture, social and local history.

The photographic collections include prints from the earliest days of photography to today's high-resolution digital images. Subjects range from Neolithic flint mines and medieval churches to art deco cinemas and 1980s shopping centres. The collection is a vivid record both of buildings that are still part of everyday life – places of work, leisure and worship – and those lost long ago, surviving only in fragile prints or glass-plate negatives.

Six million aerial photographs offer a unique and fascinating view of the transformation of England's towns, cities, coast and countryside from 1919 onwards. Highlights include the pioneering photography of Aerofilms, and the comprehensive survey of England captured by the RAF after the Second World War.

Plans, drawings and reports provide further context and reconstruction artworks bring archaeological sites and historic buildings to life.

The collections are housed in a purpose-built environmentally controlled store in Swindon, which provides the best conditions to preserve archive items for future generations to enjoy. You can search our catalogue online, see and buy copies of our images, as well as visiting our public search room by appointment.

Find out more about us at HistoricEngland.org.uk/Photos
email: archive@historicengland.org.uk
tel.: 01793 414600

The Historic England offices and archive store in Swindon from the air, 2007.